KU-574-780

Practise Your Phonics With Julia Donaldson's Songbirds

OXFORD
UNIVERSITY PRESS

OXFORD
UNIVERSITY PRESS

Great Clarendon Street, Oxford, OX2 6DP, United Kingdom

Oxford University Press is a department of the University of Oxford.
It furthers the University's objective of excellence in research, scholarship
and education by publishing worldwide. Oxford is a registered trade mark
of Oxford University Press in the UK and in certain other countries

Text © Julia Donaldson 2006
Jack and the Giants illustrations © Martin Chatterton 2006
Tara's Party illustrations © Ross Collins 2006
The Deer and the Earwig illustrations © Scoular Anderson 2006
All other illustrations © Oxford University Press 2006

The moral rights of the author have been asserted

First Edition published 2006
This Edition published 2012

All rights reserved. No part of this publication may be reproduced, stored
in a retrieval system, or transmitted, in any form or by any means, without
the prior permission in writing of Oxford University Press, or as expressly
permitted by law, by licence or under terms agreed with the appropriate
reprographics rights organization. Enquiries concerning reproduction
outside the scope of the above should be sent to the Rights Department,
Oxford University Press, at the address above.

You must not circulate this work in any other form and you must
impose this same condition on any acquirer

British Library Cataloguing in Publication Data
Data available

978-0-19-279304-1

10 9 8 7

Printed in China

Paper used in the production of this book is a natural, recyclable product
made from wood grown in sustainable forests. The manufacturing process
conforms to the environmental regulations of the country of origin.

Acknowledgements
Series editor Clare Kirtley
Art edited by Hilary Wright

Helping your child's learning
with free eBooks, essential
tips and fun activities
www.oxfordowl.co.uk

Songbirds

Tara's Party

Story by Julia Donaldson
Pictures by Ross Collins
Series editor Clare Kirtley

OXFORD
UNIVERSITY PRESS

Tips for reading Tara's Party together

This book practises these letter patterns that make the same sound:

> ar a*

Ask your child to point to these letter patterns and say the sound (e.g. *ar* as in *scarf* and *a* as in *father*). Look out for these letter patterns in the story.

Your child might find these words tricky:

> for   all   come   was   were   have   her   one   said
>
> some   the   there   they   everyone   friends   want

These words are common, but your child may not have learned how to sound them out yet. Say the words for your child if they do not know them.

Before you begin, ask your child to read the title. Remind your child to read words they do not recognise by sounding out and blending. Look at the picture together. What do you think this story is about?

When you have finished reading the story, look through it again and:

- Ask your child, *Did Martha enjoy the party?* (No.) *Why not?* (She thought everyone had been nasty to her.)
- Find some words on pages 10 and 11 which contain a long *ar* sound (*Martha, scarf, Tara's, started*). Point to the letter pattern that makes the long *ar* sound in the words (*ar*). Think of some words which rhyme with *start* and try to write them down (e.g. *cart, chart, dart, part, tart*).

*The letter *a* is pronounced *ar* in Southern England, but in the north it is pronounced *a* as in *hat*.

Tara was six.
"Can I have a party?" she asked.
"Yes," said Mum.

Tara sent cards to her friends.

Veejay came to the party.
He gave Tara a toy car.

Emma came to the party.
She gave Tara a scarf.

Martha came last.
She gave Tara one marble.

Then Martha put on the scarf.
"I want it," she said.

"It's Tara's scarf," said Emma.
Martha started to cry.

"Let's play Pass the Parcel," said Tara.
Tara passed the parcel to Veejay.

Veejay passed the parcel to Emma.

Emma passed the parcel to Martha.

Martha didn't pass the parcel.
She started to rip off all the paper.

"Pass the parcel!" said Tara.
Martha started to cry.
"I'm not playing," she said.

There were some sweets inside the parcel.
Veejay found them.

Martha started to cry again.
"I want the sweets," she said.

They had tea.
There were jam tarts and bananas.

"I'm starving," said Martha.
She ate ten jam tarts and five bananas.

"Let's play Hide and Seek," said Tara.

Veejay and Emma hid in the garden.
Tara found them.

Martha hid in the bath.
She found a lot of jars.
She took the lids off them.

Tara found Martha.
"Put the lids back on the jars," she said.

Martha started to cry again.

Emma's mum and Veejay's dad came for them.
"Was it a good party?" they asked.
"Yes," said Emma and Veejay.

Martha's mum came last.
"Was it a good party?" she asked.

"No," said Martha. "Everyone was nasty to me."

Songbirds

Paula the Vet

Story by Julia Donaldson
Pictures by Joelle Dreidemy
Series editor Clare Kirtley

OXFORD
UNIVERSITY PRESS

Tips for reading Paula the Vet together

This book practises these letter patterns that all make the same sound:

or au aw ore oor a

Ask your child to point to these letter patterns and say the sound (*au* as in *Paula*). Look out for these letter patterns in the story.

Your child might find these words tricky:

any comes girl her here the says scissors
through your

These words are common, but your child may not have learned how to sound them out yet. Say the words for your child if they do not know them.

Before you begin, ask your child to read the title. Remind your child to read words they do not recognise by sounding out and blending. Look at the picture together. What do you think this story is about?

When you have finished reading the story, look through it again and:

- Ask your child, *Which pet do you think Paula is the most interested in? Why?* (The dinosaur because it is an extraordinary pet.)

- Find some words on pages 34 and 35 which contain a long *au* sound (*Paula, paw, torn, thorn*). Point to the letter pattern that makes the long *au* sound in the words (*au, aw, or*). Identify which of these words rhyme (*torn, thorn*). Think of some more words which rhyme with *torn* (e.g. *born, corn, dawn, horn, lawn*.)

Paula is a vet
and a very good vet.
She opens the door
and she calls, "Next pet!"

Here comes a man.
He walks through the door.

He says, "My cat
has a very sore paw."

Paula has a look.
The paw is torn.

"Aha!" says Paula,
and takes out a thorn.

Yes, Paula is a vet
and a very good vet.
She opens the door
and she calls, "Next pet!"

Here comes a boy.
He walks through the door.
He says, "My little dog's
tummy is sore."

Paula tells the boy,
"Your dog is ill,
but she'll soon get better
if she takes this pill."

Yes, Paula is a vet
and a very good vet.
She opens the door
and she calls, "Next pet!"

Here comes a lady.
She walks through the door.
She says, "My rabbit
has a very long claw."

Paula tells the lady,
"The nail needs a clip."
Paula gets her scissors –
snip, snip, snip!

Yes, Paula is a vet
and a very good vet.
She opens the door
and she calls, "Next pet!"

Here comes a girl.
She walks through the door.
She says, "My mouse
won't run any more."

Paula has a look,
and she says, "I think
your mouse just needs
more water to drink."

46

All the morning,
Paula the vet
sees pet,

after pet,

after pet,

after pet.

More and more dogs,

more and more cats,

more and more rabbits

and mice

and rats.

Paula sees ordinary pets
all morning.
Paula feels bored.
Paula starts yawning.

"It's always the same,"
thinks Paula the vet.
"I wish I could see an
extraordinary pet!"

But Paula the vet
is a very good vet.
So she opens the door
and she calls, "Next pet!"

Here comes someone.
He walks through the door.
It's a very small boy. . .

with a **dinosaur!**

Songbirds

Where Were You, Bert?

Story by Julia Donaldson
Pictures by Richard Watson
Series editor Clare Kirtley

OXFORD
UNIVERSITY PRESS

Tips for reading Where Were You, Bert? together

This book practises these letter patterns that all make the same sound:

er ir ur ear

Ask your child to point to these letter patterns and say the sound (e.g. *ur* as in *fur*). Look out for these letter patterns in the story.

Your child might find these words tricky:

some was Where you you're

These words are common, but your child may not have learned how to sound them out yet. Say the words for your child if they do not know them.

Before you begin, ask your child to read the title. Remind your child to read words they do not recognise by sounding out and blending. Look at the picture together. What do you think this story is about?

When you have finished reading the story, look through it again and:

● Ask your child, *Why was Bert early at the end of the story?* (He didn't want to do lots of extra work.)

● Find some words on pages 59 and 60 which contain the long *ur* sound (*Bert, Sir, were, Er, her, purse*). Point to the letter pattern that makes the long *ur* sound in these words (*er, ir, ere, ur*). Point out that *were* is a common word with an unusual spelling pattern for the *ur* sound.

"You're late, Bert!"
"Sorry, Sir."
"Where were you, Bert?"

"Er...I was helping a little girl to find her mummy."

"You're late again, Bert!"
"Sorry, Sir."
"Where were you, Bert?"

"Er...I was helping a lady to find her purse."

"You're late again, Bert!"
"Sorry, Sir."
"Where were you, Bert?"

"Er...I was helping a furry caterpillar to find a leaf."

"You're late again, Bert!"
"Sorry, Sir."
"Where were you, Bert?"

"Er…I was helping a thirsty dog to find a drink."

"You're late again, Bert!"
"Sorry, Sir ."
"Where were you, Bert?"

"Er…I was helping a little boy to find a birthday party."

"You're late again, Bert!"
"Sorry, Sir."
"Where were you, Bert?"

"Er...I was helping a bird to find its nest."

"You're late again, Bert!"
"Sorry, Sir."
"Where were you, Bert?"

"Er...I was helping a worm to find some earth."

"You're late again, Bert!"
"Sorry, Sir."
"Where were you, Bert?"

"Er...I was helping a nurse to find her hospital."

"You're late again, Bert!"
"Sorry, Sir."
"Where were you, Bert?"

"Er...I was helping a turtle to find a pond."

"You're late again, Bert!"
"Sorry, Sir."
"Where were you, Bert?"

"Er…I was helping a mermaid to find a pearl."

"You're late again, Bert!"
"Sorry, Sir."
"Where were you, Bert?"

"Er...I was helping a clown to find the circus."

"Don't be late again, Bert!"
"No, Sir."
"If you're late again, Bert, I will help you find a lot of extra work."

"You're early, Bert!"

Songbirds

Clare and the Fair

Story by Julia Donaldson
Pictures by Barbara Vagnozzi
Series editor Clare Kirtley

OXFORD
UNIVERSITY PRESS

Tips for reading Clare and the Fair together

This book practises these letter patterns that all make the same sound:

air are ear

Ask your child to point to these letter patterns and say the sound (e.g. *air* as in *fair*). Look out for these letter patterns in the story.

Your child might find these words tricky:

are come have everyone's everywhere the
their there was

These words are common, but your child may not have learned how to sound them out yet. Say the words for your child if they do not know them.

Before you begin, ask your child to read the title. Remind your child to read words they do not recognise by sounding out and blending. Look at the picture together. What do you think this story is about?

When you have finished reading the story, look through it again and:

- Ask your child, *What would they like to do at the fair? Why?*
- Find some words on pages 91, 92 and 93 which rhyme (*scare, bear, fair*). Identify what sound is the same in all these words? (*the end sound air*) On pages 98 and 99 find some more words which contain the long *air* sound. (*Clare, there, hair*) Point out that *there* is a common word with an unusual spelling pattern for the *air* sound.

Clare and the Fair
Two Poems

Come to the Fair

Come to the fair!
Come to the fair!

Ride in a car.

Ride in a chair.

Down to the ground and
up in the air!

Mums, dads and children
– everyone's there,
flying around with
the wind in their hair.

Have a good stare.

You might win a fairy.
You might win a bear.

So come to the fair!
Come to the fair!

Clare! Clare!

"Clare, Clare! Look over there!
Who has spilt cornflakes all over the
chair ?

Did you do it, Clare?"

"Oh no," said Clare.
"I didn't do it. It was my bear."

"Clare! Clare! Look over there!

Poor little Mary has jam in her hair!

Did you do it, Clare?"

"Oh no," said Clare.
"I didn't do it. It was my bear."

"Clare! Clare! Look over there!
Jars, tins and packets are everywhere.

Did you do it, Clare?"
"Oh no," said Clare.
"I didn't do it. It was my bear."

"Bear, Bear! Look over there!
Who has been giving the kitten a scare?

Did you do it, Bear?"
"Oh no," said Bear.
"I didn't do it.

It must have been Clare."

Songbirds

The Deer and the Earwig

Story by Julia Donaldson
Pictures by Scoular Anderson
Series editor Clare Kirtley

OXFORD
UNIVERSITY PRESS

Tips for reading The Deer and the Earwig together

This book practises these letter patterns that all make the same sound:

ear   eer   ere

Ask your child to point to these letter patterns and say the sound (e.g. *eer* as in *cheer*). Look out for these letter patterns in the story.

Your child might find these words tricky:

climbs   comes   says

These words are common, but your child may not have learned how to sound them out yet. Say the words for your child if they do not know them.

Before you begin, ask your child to read the title. Remind your child to read words they do not recognise by sounding out and blending. Look at the picture together. What do you think this story is about?

When you have finished reading the story, look through it again and:

- Ask your child, *How did the earwig save the deer?* (He bit the hunter's ear which made him drop the spear and the deer ran away.)
- Find some words on pages 111 and 112 which rhyme (*hear, ear, cheer*). Point to the letter pattern that makes the long *ear* sound in these words. Find some more words on page 125 which contain the long *ear* sound (*dear, Here, spear*). Point to the letter pattern that makes the long *ear* sound in these words (*ear, ere, ear*).

The Deer and the Earwig
A Poem and a Story

I Hear with my Little Ear

I hear with my little ear . . .

Hooray! Hooray!
A very loud cheer.

I hear with my little ear . . .

A very loud **bump**!
(My dad can't steer.)

I hear with my little ear . . .

A snap of twigs.

It's a very shy deer.

The Deer and the Earwig

Here is a stream. Here is a deer.

And here is a little black earwig.

Oh dear! The earwig has fallen into
the stream!
"Help! Help!" he cries.

"Do not fear, I am here," says the deer.
She drops a leaf into the stream.

The earwig climbs on to the leaf.
He sails to the bank.

"Thank you, deer," says the earwig.
"You saved my life."

A week later. . .
Here is the stream. Here is the deer.
And here is the little black earwig.

Oh dear! Here is a hunter!
He has a spear.

The deer can't see the hunter.
She can't hear him.

Help! The hunter lifts his spear.

But here comes the earwig.

"Do not fear, I am here!" he says.

The earwig nips the hunter's ear.
The hunter jumps and drops the spear.

The deer runs away.

"Thank you, earwig," says the deer.
"You saved my life."

Songbirds

Jack
and the Giants

Story by Julia Donaldson
Pictures by Martin Chatterton
Series editor Clare Kirtley

OXFORD
UNIVERSITY PRESS

Tips for reading Jack and the Giants together

This book practises these letter patterns:

> ure   our   (all pronounced ure as in pure)

> ea   e   (all pronounced ea as in sea)

> e   ea   (all pronounced e as in get)

> ow   (pronounced ow as in how)

> ow   (pronounced ow as in slow)

> j   g   dge   (all pronounced j as in just)

Ask your child to point to these letter patterns and say the sounds (e.g. *ow* as in *how*). Look out for these letter patterns in the story.

Your child might find these words tricky:

> are   coming   guide   the   there   they   want   what   where   you

These words are common, but your child may not have learned how to sound them out yet. Say the words for your child if they do not know them.

Before you begin, ask your child to read the title. Remind your child to read words they do not recognise by sounding out and blending. Look at the picture together. What do you think this story is about? When you have finished reading the story, look through it again and:

- Ask your child, *Why do the giants think some things are cute and little?*
- Read what Jack says on pages 133 and 141. Find two words which contain the letter pattern *ow* (*follow, town*). Say what sound the letter pattern makes in each word. Stress that the same letter pattern can make different sounds.

Jack and the Giants
A Play

The Characters

Mum
Dad } *three giant tourists*
Midge

Jack   *a tour guide*

Jack: Hello, giants. I'm Jack, and I'm going to show you round the town.

Mum: Hello, Jack!

Dad: Hello, Jack!

Midge: He is so cute!

Jack: Are you ready to go on the tour?

Giants: Yes, we are!

Jack: Please be sure not to tread on me!
Mum: Did you hear that, Midge?
Midge: Yes, Mum.

Jack: Off we go then! Follow me, please, giants.

Dad: What a cute little village!

Mum: No, you can't.

Jack: Now, this is the art gallery.
Dad: Look at those cute little stamps!

Jack: They are not stamps. They are big pictures!

Midge: Can I put them in my doll's house?

Dad: No, you can't.

Jack: Now, this is the zoo.

Midge: Look at that cute little kitten!

Jack: It's not a kitten. It's a huge tiger!

Mum: Look at that cute little creature with the thin little neck!

Jack: That's a giraffe!

Midge: Is there a gift shop, Dad?

Dad: I don't know. Let's ask Jack.

Mum: Where is Jack?

Dad: Yes, where is he?

Mum: I hope you didn't tread on him, Midge.

Jack: Let me out! Let me out!

Dad: I can hear his cute little voice!

Jack: Let me out!

Mum: It's coming from your pocket, Midge.

155

Jack: Put me down!

Dad: Yes, put him down, Midge!

Midge: But I want to take him back and put him in my doll's house.

Mum: Well you can't.

Jack: The tour is over!

Practise Your Phonics With
Julia Donaldson's
Songbirds

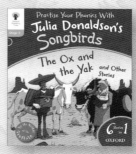

By the Author of The **Gruffalo**

Look out for the other titles in the series ...

Top Cat and Other Stories
978-0-19-279296-9

The Odd Pet and Other Stories
978-0-19-279297-6

The Ox and the Yak and Other Stories
978-0-19-279298-3

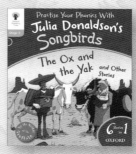

Scrap Rocket and Other Stories
978-0-19-279299-0

Where is the Snail? and Other Stories
978-0-19-279300-3

Tadpoles and Other Stories
978-0-19-279301-0

My Cat and Other Stories
978-0-19-279302-7

Leroy and Other Stories
978-0-19-279303-4

Where Were You Bert? and Other Stories
978-0-19-279304-1

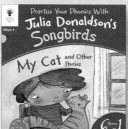

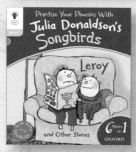

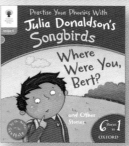